Ruth Bader Ginsburg

by Laurie Calkhoven

illustrated by Elizabet Vukovic

Ready-to-Read

Simon Spotlight
New York   London   Toronto   Sydney   New Delhi

SIMON SPOTLIGHT
An imprint of Simon & Schuster Children's Publishing Division
1230 Avenue of the Americas, New York, New York 10020
This Simon Spotlight edition December 2020
Text copyright © 2019 by Simon & Schuster, Inc.
Illustrations copyright © 2019 by Elizabet Vukovic
For information about special discounts for bulk purchases, please contact Simon & Schuster Special Sales at
1-866-506-1949 or business@simonandschuster.com.
Manufactured in China 0920 LEO

CONTENTS

Introduction

Have you ever wanted to make the world a better place? Or seen people being treated unfairly and wanted to help? If so, then you should meet Ruth Bader Ginsburg.

In 1993, Ruth Bader Ginsburg became the second female Supreme Court justice in American history. But before that, she had to fight to become a lawyer at a time when many people believed it was a job only men should do.

As a lawyer, Ruth argued legal cases to make sure women were treated equally in the courts and in the workplace.

Over the years she became such a strong voice for what she believed in that people started calling her the "Notorious R.B.G.," after a rap and hip-hop artist (the Notorious B.I.G.) who was also from Brooklyn. **Notorious** means "widely known," sometimes for something bad. In Ruth's case, it's because she fights for what she believes in.

Once you meet Ruth Bader Ginsburg, you'll understand why!

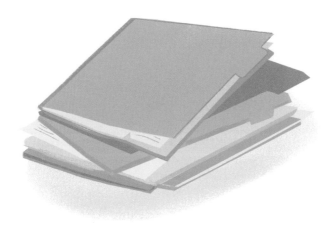

Chapter 1
Brooklyn Born

Ruth Bader was born on March 15, 1933, in Brooklyn, New York. Her parents, who were both Jewish, came from families that had left Europe to escape anti-Jewish persecution.

Ruth's father, Nathan, was a furrier. He never finished high school. Her mother, Celia, earned top grades. She would have liked to go to college. Celia's family didn't think it was necessary to educate girls. At that time, most girls got married and raised children and didn't work outside the home. Instead of going to college herself, Celia went to work to help pay for her brother's education.

Ruth's mother never forgot how much she had wanted to go to college. She encouraged Ruth to get as much education as she could. She told her daughter stories about taking part in suffrage parades twenty years before. The word **suffrage** means "the right to vote in political elections." Suffrage parades were marches

to win women the right to vote. She
wanted Ruth to have more opportunities
than she'd had.

Celia loved to read, and she passed on
that love to her daughter. Every week, she
dropped Ruth off at the local library. Ruth
liked to read books about mythology. She
also enjoyed Nancy Drew novels and wanted
to be brave and adventurous like Nancy.

Ruth was a top student in high school. She liked to keep busy! Ruth edited the school newspaper, twirled a baton, and learned to play cello. She loved music, especially opera.

Those activities kept Ruth busy. However, things were sad at home. Her mother had cancer and was very sick. Ruth often did homework at her mother's bedside. That made her mother happy.

Ruth was chosen to make a speech at her high school graduation. Sadly, her mother died the night before. Instead of walking across the stage to accept her diploma, Ruth planned a funeral with her father.

As sad as she was, Ruth knew her mother wanted her to go to college. She had earned a scholarship to Cornell University. In September 1950, she set off to fulfill her and her mother's dream of getting a college education.

Chapter 2
College Dreams

Ruth's mother wasn't like the typical mother back then. At a time when one of the only options for girls was to marry and be homemakers, Celia believed Ruth could do anything she set her mind to. She had given her daughter two pieces of advice. The first was to be a lady. That meant she didn't want Ruth to give in to emotions like anger or jealousy. The second was to be independent. She told Ruth it would be great if "Prince Charming" came along, but she should be ready to take care of herself.

Ruth took those two pieces of advice to Cornell with her.

Bathroom

Bathroom

College girls weren't encouraged to work hard. But Ruth wanted to study! She learned where all the women's bathrooms were on campus and often snuck inside one to study unseen. But studying didn't stop her from making friends and going on dates.

Ruth was still a freshman when she went on a blind date with Martin "Marty" Ginsburg. Marty, Ruth said later, was the first boy "who cared that I had a brain."

The two made a good team. Ruth was shy and quiet; Marty was outgoing. They both decided to be lawyers. Ruth wanted to use the law to help people.

The couple was married a few days after Ruth graduated from Cornell with a degree in government in 1954. Marty had just finished his first year at Harvard Law School. Ruth planned to join him there in September. Then Marty got drafted into the army, and the couple's law school plans were postponed. In the meantime, they had a daughter named Jane. Finally, in the fall of 1956, Ruth entered Harvard Law School. Ruth was one of just nine women in a class of five hundred students.

One night, the **dean** invited those nine women to his house for dinner. (The dean is the head of the law school.) He went around the table and made each woman tell him why she deserved a place at the law school when that spot could have gone to a man. He made the women feel as if he

really didn't want them there. Ruth didn't know how to answer. She knew in those days it wasn't considered feminine to want to work outside the home. She told the dean that she wanted to be able to discuss her husband's work with him during dinner when he came home at the end of the day.

That wasn't the only time Ruth felt unwelcome at law school. Once, she needed an article from a certain room in the law library. A guard wouldn't allow her in. He said the room was only open to men.

Ruth remembered her mother's advice and didn't give in to anger. She earned good grades. She kept that up even in her second year when Marty was diagnosed with cancer. She took care of Marty and their daughter, Jane, and made sure Marty got notes from all his classes. He graduated because of Ruth's help. When Marty's health improved, he got a job in New York City. Ruth transferred to Columbia Law School and tied for first in her class.

There was just one problem. Once again, no one wanted to hire her because she was a woman.

Chapter 3
Professor Ginsburg

Ruth had graduated at the top of her law school class, but not one law firm in New York City wanted to hire her. The men who ran the law firms didn't believe that a woman, especially a mother, could do the job as well as a man.

One of Ruth's professors tried to get her a job as a law clerk. A law clerk is an assistant to a judge. A clerk's responsibility is to do legal research and provide general assistance. Two judges turned him down because they didn't want to hire a woman. The third one said yes. Ruth turned out to be one of his best clerks ever. Her research was always very thorough, and she met every deadline.

Ruth later went on to become a professor at Rutgers Law School. When she learned that she was pregnant with her second child, her son, James, she kept it a secret by wearing baggier clothes. At the time, pregnant women were discouraged from working. Many were fired.

Women across the country were getting tired of being treated unfairly by the law

and by their employers. They wanted the same chances to succeed that men had. They wanted to earn the same money that men did for doing the same jobs.

Ruth worked with the American Civil Liberties Union (ACLU) to start the Women's Rights Project. Ruth was going to fight for women's rights in the courts.

Chapter 4
The Women's Rights Project

Ruth chose her cases for the Women's Rights Project very carefully. She looked for cases that would prove to the courts that laws that treated men and women unequally were bad for everyone. Because those cases challenged laws that had been in effect for a long time, many of them ended up at the Supreme Court—the highest court in the United States.

In January 1973, Ruth argued her first case before the nine male justices of the Supreme Court. Ruth was so nervous, she didn't eat lunch that day! Wearing her mother's earrings and circle pin for luck, she argued that laws treating men and women differently were unfair.

RUTH BADER GINSBURG
FIGHTS FOR WOMEN

GINSBURG

GINSBURG WINS CASE
FOR EQUAL RIGHTS

In her argument, Ruth quoted Sarah
Grimké, a woman who'd fought hard to
win the right to vote. "All I ask of our
brethren," Ruth quoted, "is that they

take their feet off our necks." In other words, Ruth wanted men to stop holding women back.

Ruth won her case! She went on to argue five more legal cases before the Supreme Court, wearing her mother's circle pin and earrings each time. She won four of the cases. She also helped write the arguments for many other successful cases. Her family was so proud of her, especially her children.

EQUAL RIGHTS CASE HITS HOME FOR RUTH BADER GINSBURG

Ruth's children weren't the only ones who were impressed by their mother's thinking. President Jimmy Carter also heard about Ruth's keen legal mind. He asked Ruth to be a judge on the US Court of Appeals, the second-highest court in the United States. She soon had a reputation for being fair-minded. Thirteen years later, in 1993, when there was an opening on the Supreme Court, President Bill Clinton turned to Ruth and nominated her for the position.

She would become the second woman in history, and the first Jewish woman, to sit on the highest court in the United States. (In 1981, Sandra Day O'Connor was the first woman appointed to the Supreme Court.)

Chapter 5
You Can't Spell "Truth" without Ruth!

Ruth stood next to President Clinton in the Rose Garden of the White House to accept the nomination to the Supreme Court in 1993. She was wearing her mother's circle pin and earrings.

In more than twenty-five years on the Supreme Court, Ruth earned a reputation as a brilliant legal mind. She's also known for her famous friendships with people who don't always agree with her. More recently, though, she has become known for her **dissents**.

In order to win a Supreme Court case, five or more of the nine justices have to agree. They are the **majority**. Those that disagree with the majority—the **minority**—have an opportunity to explain why they disagree. These are called dissents.

After President George W. Bush appointed two new justices to the bench in

the 2000s, Ruth often found herself in the minority. More and more often, she could be heard saying, "I dissent."

People began to love Ruth for her dissents. That's when people started calling her the Notorious R.B.G. Other people took up the slogan "You Can't Spell 'Truth' without Ruth."

Ruth is also known for the fancy collars she wears with her black robes. People who follow the Supreme Court know that if she is wearing the collar with the gold trim and charms, she's part of the majority opinion. She wears her glass-beaded velvet collar for dissents. And she has many other collars to wear when listening to legal arguments.

Ruth has battled cancer three times. After the first time, she started exercising to stay strong. During her treatments, she rarely missed a day's work. Many people have asked Ruth, who turned eighty-six

in 2019, when she will retire. Her answer is always the same. As long as she can still do her job, she will remain on the Supreme Court.

The Notorious R.B.G. will never stop fighting to make the world a better place. Now that you've met her, don't you want to do the same?

BUT WAIT . . .

THERE'S MORE!

Turn the page to learn more about Ruth Bader Ginsburg's life and the Supreme Court.

Did You Know?

Ruth thinks it's important to maintain a healthy workout routine. She is in her eighties and works out with a personal trainer twice a week and can do up to twenty push-ups!

Ruth loves listening to opera music. One of her all-time favorite operas is called *The Marriage of Figaro* composed by Mozart.

Ruth learned Swedish to coauthor a book, *Civil Procedure in Sweden*, with Anders Bruzelius. Ruth learned Swedish because she didn't want anything she said in the book to be incorrectly translated. The book is about civil legal procedure in Sweden.

The Supreme Court

The Supreme Court is the highest court in the United States. The court's job is to uphold the laws of the nation.

The president of the United States nominates Supreme Court justices, and the Senate confirms them. Once they are accepted, they hold their office for life.

The Supreme Court's motto is "Equal Justice Under Law."

To date, only four women have served as justices on the Supreme Court of the United States (SCOTUS): Sandra Day O'Connor, Sonia Sotomayor, Ruth Bader Ginsburg, and Elena Kagan.

Women on the Supreme Court

Currently there are three women on the Supreme Court: Ruth Bader Ginsburg, Sonia Sotomayor, and Elena Kagan. You've already read about Ruth; now read a little bit about the other two amazing women currently on our Supreme Court!

Justice Sonia Sotomayor

Sonia was born in the Bronx in New York. She was nominated to the Supreme Court by President Barack Obama on May 26, 2009, and became the first Latina Supreme Court justice in US history. She attended Princeton University and initially felt overwhelmed and

received a low grade on her first midterm paper. This only made her more determined to study harder and do better, and her hard work paid off in the end. She graduated summa cum laude (with highest distinction) from Princeton in 1976. She was also awarded the Pyne Prize, which is the highest academic award given to Princeton undergraduate students. Sonia has become well-known for her legal battles against discrimination, and for demanding equal rights and representation for all.

Justice Elena Kagan

Elena was born in New York City, New York. She was nominated by President Barack Obama to the Supreme Court on May 10, 2010. Elena was introduced to the practice of law at an early age, as her dad was a partner at the law firm Kagan & Lubic. She attended Princeton University; the University of Oxford in Oxford, England; and Harvard Law School, where she graduated magna cum laude (with great distinction) in 1986. Before her nomination to the Supreme Court, President Obama chose Elena for the role of solicitor general. The United 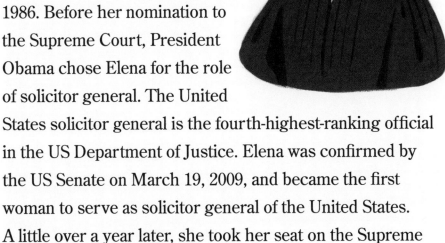 States solicitor general is the fourth-highest-ranking official in the US Department of Justice. Elena was confirmed by the US Senate on March 19, 2009, and became the first woman to serve as solicitor general of the United States. A little over a year later, she took her seat on the Supreme Court on August 7, 2010.

By the Numbers

 The Supreme Court began with only six justices.

As of 2019, there are now eight associate justices on the court and one chief justice. Currently six are men and three are women.

 The court receives more than seven thousand cases to review each year. They typically agree to hear about eighty cases during the year.

The longest-serving justice on the Supreme Court was William O. Douglas, who served thirty-six years, seven months, and eight days in office.

Martin Ginsburg

Martin "Marty" Ginsburg was Ruth's husband. They were married from June 23, 1954, until his death on June 27, 2010. That's fifty-six years!

They had two children together: Jane Carol Ginsburg and James Steven Ginsburg.

Marty had a major impact on Ruth's life and work. When Ruth started arguing cases before the Supreme Court, Marty took over at home. After tasting Ruth's awful tuna noodle casserole early in their marriage, he realized that he had better learn to cook! Many years later, Ruth's daughter, Jane, joked, "My father did the cooking, and my mother did the thinking!"

Ruth once wrote of Marty: "I betray no secret in reporting that, without him, I would not have gained a seat on the Supreme Court."

She also said, "I have had more than a little bit of luck in life, but nothing equals in magnitude my marriage to Martin D. Ginsburg. I do not have words adequate to describe my supersmart, exuberant, ever-loving spouse."

Now that you've met Ruth, what have you learned?

1. How many Supreme Court justices serve on the court today?
a. nine   b. six   c. seven   d. ten

2. Ruth wears her gold-trimmed collar when she opposes a decision on the court.
a. true   b. false

3. What advice did Ruth's mother give her?
a. to get as much education as she desired
b. to never give in to anger or jealousy
c. to be independent
d. all of the above

4. What type of entertainment does Ruth enjoy the most?
a. theater   b. opera   c. piano concerts   d. movies

5. When was Ruth appointed as a Supreme Court justice?
a. 1972   b. 1954   c. 1993   d. 1965

6. Where did Ruth study?
a. Harvard Law School   b. Cornell University
c. Rutgers Law School   d. A and B

7. Which president nominated Ruth to the Supreme Court?
a. Bill Clinton   b. George W. Bush
c. Barack Obama   d. Jimmy Carter

8. Ruth Bader Ginsburg was the first woman to serve on the Supreme Court.
a. true   b. false

9. Why did Ruth choose her cases carefully?
a. She wanted to show how smart she was.
b. She wanted to prove men and women should be treated equally.
c. She wanted to be famous.
d. She wanted people to like her.

10. What is Ruth known for wearing?
a. a lucky bracelet   b. her mother's necklace
c. fancy collars   d. ruby earrings

Answers: 1.a 2.b 3.d 4.b 5.c 6.d 7.a 8.b 9.b 10.c